Royal Wedding Dresses

Nigel Arch & Joanna Marschner

Contents

Left:
Princess Elizabeth and the Duke of Edinburgh on their wedding day, 20 November 1947.

Right:
Princess Margaret leaving Clarence House for Westminster Abbey on her wedding day, 6 May 1960.

Introduction

At every wedding the visual focus is always the dress, and a royal wedding is no different. In the midst of all the pomp and splendour all eyes are on the bride; her gown feverishly anticipated and endlessly discussed. This is the story of ten royal wedding dresses, which span nearly 200 years. Five of them are part of the unique Royal Ceremonial Dress Collection at Kensington Palace.

Changes in the customs and practices of weddings inevitably reflect changes in society. Arranged marriages designed to consolidate property and power give way to unions in which sentiment and relationship have greater weight.

So too with royal weddings: state diplomacy yields to love. Although mutual attraction was important – between, for example, Princess Charlotte and Leopold of Saxe-Coburg and Queen Victoria and Prince Albert – the balance of power in Europe continued to be an important factor in the marriage choices of Victoria's children. Now, of course, the idea of the two young people not being deeply in love from the start strikes us as extraordinary.

There is another characteristic of royal weddings that marks them out from the weddings of the monarch's subjects: almost universally they are the focus of national celebration. Huge crowds lined The Mall for Princess Charlotte's wedding in 1816 and thousands cheered Queen Victoria as she left Buckingham Palace for the Chapel Royal at St James's Palace in February 1840, although they did so amid torrents of rain. So it continued: Princess Alexandra arrived from Denmark for her wedding with the Prince of Wales in 1861 and drove in an open carriage through streets strewn with garlands and banners. In the 20th century first film – in 1923 for the wedding of the Duke and Duchess of York – and then television – in 1960 for Princess Margaret's marriage to Antony Armstrong-Jones – took the spectacle to an international stage. In 2011 it was claimed that an estimated 2 billion people across the globe had watched the wedding of Prince William and Catherine Middleton – making it possibly one of the most popular programmes ever broadcast.

The Prince and Princess of Wales leaving St Paul's Cathedral after their wedding ceremony, 29 July 1981.

Princess Charlotte

(1796-1817)

Right:
Princess Charlotte Augusta of Wales by Richard Woodman, c1816. In this portrait the Princess is shown wearing her wedding ring and the diamond bracelet given to her as a wedding gift by her husband.

The nation rejoiced at the wedding of this popular princess, but her happiness was cut tragically short.

Princess Charlotte was the daughter of George, Prince of Wales (later King George IV) and Caroline of Brunswick. Their marriage was an unhappy one and Charlotte was an only child. In order for the dynasty to continue, Charlotte had to marry and produce an heir to the throne. On 2 May 1816 she married Leopold of Saxe-Coburg at Carlton House in London.

The Princess's wedding dress comprised a petticoat of white and silver, worn under a net dress embroidered with silver lamé. There was a deep border of embroidered flowers forming festoons around the hem. The neck and sleeves were trimmed with Brussels lace while her train was in the same silver and white material as the underdress and ornamented to match. The Princess's jewellery included a headdress of rosebuds and leaves formed from diamonds and a pair of large drop earrings.

The wedding was celebrated on an enormous scale. There were grand balls throughout the country and people were able to buy commemorative wares; in fact it was the first royal marriage of which souvenirs were so widely available. Sadly, the hopes engendered by the occasion were not to be fulfilled. In November 1817, the Princess died in childbirth, having been delivered of a stillborn son. With no heir to the throne, it fell to the Prince of Wales's brothers to marry and produce sons and daughters who could assume this role. One of these brothers, Edward, Duke of Kent, had a daughter, Princess Alexandrina Victoria, who duly came to the throne in 1837 as Queen Victoria.

Above:
Princess Charlotte and Prince Leopold in 1816.

Below:
Princess Charlotte's wedding dress, 1816.

Queen Victoria

(1819-1901)

We have Queen Victoria to thank for introducing the custom of wearing orange blossom as a bride. Her simple white dress set a pattern for royal wedding style that survives to this day.

The marriage of Queen Victoria and Prince Albert marked the culmination of family plans hatched many years earlier. When the two royal babies were still in their respective cradles the Dowager Duchess of Saxe-Coburg and Gotha had remarked of Prince Albert, 'what a charming pendant he would be to his pretty cousin'. The intervening years had seen many changes in family circumstances, not least the accession of Princess Victoria to the throne of Great Britain on 20 June 1837, following the death of her uncle, King William IV.

Queen Victoria's initial 'great repugnance' to the discussion of her future marriage plans was utterly swept away in October 1839 with the arrival in London of Prince Albert 'who is beautiful'. On 15 October Prince Albert was called into the Queen's presence where, as laid down by protocol, she proposed to him. She later recorded in her journal: 'I said to him that I thought he must be aware why I wished him to come here – and that it would make me happy if he would consent to what I wished'.

With the date of the wedding quickly settled, Lord Melbourne, the Prime Minister, hastened to research the protocol that had surrounded earlier weddings of a reigning monarch. The Queen, however, chose to diverge in several important respects from earlier models, especially in the matter of dress: 'Talked of wearing my robes at the wedding, which I wished not', recorded the Queen in her journal, following a discussion with Lord Melbourne. She chose instead to wear a fashionable white, silk satin court dress. This much simpler style would set a pattern for royal

Above:
Queen Victoria's wedding dress, 1840.

Right:
This gold and porcelain orange blossom brooch was designed by Prince Albert as an engagement present for Queen Victoria.

8

Queen Victoria by Franz Xaver Winterhalter, 1847 (detail). This portrait was given to Prince Albert by the Queen on their seventh wedding anniversary. The Queen is shown wearing her wedding veil, her wreath of orange blossom and the sapphire brooch given to her by the Prince on the eve of their wedding.

THE PROCESSION OF QUEEN VICTORIA & PRINCE ALBERT,
THROUGH QUEEN ANNE'S DRAWING ROOM ST JAMES'S PALACE,
ON THEIR RETURN FROM THE CHAPEL ROYAL ON THE DAY OF THEIR MARRIAGE. FEBRY 10TH 1840

Above:
After the wedding ceremony, each of the 12 bridesmaids was presented with a turquoise eagle brooch, made to the designs of Prince Albert.

Above left:
Queen Victoria, Prince Albert and their bridesmaids at St James's Palace following their wedding ceremony. The Queen designed the bridesmaids' dresses herself and recorded in her journal that they 'had a beautiful effect'.

Left:
This diamond and ruby ring was a wedding present to Queen Victoria from her half-sister, Feodora. It is inscribed in French 'united forever'.

Below:
Sir George Hayter, *The Marriage of Queen Victoria and Prince Albert*, 10 February 1840 (detail).

wedding dress, which survives to this day. The bodice had a low, round neck and short, full sleeves gathered into double puffs. Edging the neckline, sleeves and the sharply-pointed waist were narrow rows of piping. The fullness of the skirt was taken in at the waist in a series of deep pleats. A court train was made of the same silk satin. It measured 6 yards in length and had a border of orange blossom sprays, matching the garland the young Queen would wear round her head. The custom of wearing these flowers for weddings took hold in Britain in the early 19th century, superseding the tradition of wearing roses, as Princess Charlotte had done on her wedding day.

It was of concern to Queen Victoria and her advisers that the entire bridal outfit should comprise materials of British manufacture. Accordingly, the silk satin was obtained from Spitalfields, in London. Mrs Bettans, the Queen's dressmaker, had the task of making the dress, which was eventually trimmed with a spectacular set of English Honiton lace made under the supervision of Miss Jane Bidney, 'lace manufacturer in ordinary to the Queen'. Miss Bidney returned to her native village of Beer in Devon in order to better undertake her commission, employing more than 200 workers between March and November 1839.

At midday on 10 February 1840, amidst 'torrents of rain, and violent gusts of wind', the Queen's procession left Buckingham Palace for the Chapel Royal at St James's Palace, where the wedding was to take place. The route was lined with thousands of people who had clambered on chairs and even into the trees to get a better view.

As Prince Albert alighted at St James's Palace, it was observed that 'he was dressed in the uniform of a British field marshal and wore no other decorations than the insignia of the Order of the Garter'. (This honour – admission to the oldest order of knighthood in Britain – had been conferred on him on 23 January of that year.) He was supported by his father, the Duke of Saxe-Coburg and Gotha, and his brother, the Hereditary Prince. 'The Duke was dressed in a dark blue uniform turned up with red and military boots similar to that worn by the Life Guards…the Collar of the Order of the Garter and Star, and the Star of the Order of Coburg Gotha. Prince Ernest wore a light blue cavalry uniform with silver appointments, carrying a light helmet in his hand…the insignia of a Grand Cross of the Order of Knighthood'.

The Chapel Royal was crowded with guests, and while court dresses and uniforms were prescribed, ladies had been especially requested not to wear court trains in order to relieve congestion. At last, to a fanfare of trumpets, the bride's procession entered, with Lord Melbourne in his new full-dress coat 'built like a seventy-four gun ship' at its head. The Queen, her dress adorned with the Collar and Star of the Garter and a sapphire and diamond brooch, a gift from Prince Albert, was supported by her uncle, the Duke of Sussex (her father having died in 1820), and followed by a flock of trainbearers, wearing dresses designed by the Queen herself.

It was barely 15 minutes later when guns boomed out over St James's Park to announce that the rings had been exchanged and, by five minutes past one o'clock, the procession had set out for Buckingham Palace, where the register was signed and the wedding breakfast consumed. *The Times* reported: 'we are assured that not one of the cherubs on the royal wedding cake was intended to represent Lord Palmerston [the Foreign Secretary, later Prime Minister]. The resemblance therefore pointed out… must be purely accidental'. At four o'clock Queen Victoria and Prince Albert drove away to Windsor. 'I and Albert alone…which was so delightful!' said the Queen.

Right:
Queen Victoria's Honiton lace
wedding flounce, 1840 (detail).

Queen Alexandra

(1844-1925)

Two years after the death of Prince Albert, Princess Alexandra of Denmark married Albert Edward, Prince of Wales. Despite the deep, almost suffocating grief of her mother-in-law, nothing could detract from the beautiful young bride.

The happiness Queen Victoria and Prince Albert derived from their marriage, and their blissfully happy memories of the wedding day itself, caused it to be established as a model for the weddings of each of their nine children.

Their eldest child, Victoria, Princess Royal, married Prince Frederick William of Prussia in January 1858, at a suitably pretty and light-hearted ceremony. However, on 14 December 1861, shortly before the wedding of their second daughter, Princess Alice, Prince Albert died of typhoid at Windsor Castle. The Queen and the whole of the royal family were devastated and the country was plunged into mourning. Princess Alice's wedding was postponed and it was not until July 1862 that she married Prince Louis of Hesse, at a simple ceremony, which was 'as private as possible'.

Despite national mourning, it was difficult to suppress the great public interest in the wedding of the heir to the throne – Albert Edward, Prince of Wales. The almost suffocating grief of Queen Victoria, however, continued unabated. Her response to her daughter Victoria's enthusiastic support of the match proposed between Albert and Princess Alexandra of Denmark was 'Dear child! Your ecstasy at the whole thing is to me very incomprehensible'. The date of the wedding was settled at 10 March 1863 and St George's Chapel, Windsor Castle was selected as the venue. The news was greeted with some surprise – the chapel had last seen a royal wedding (that of the Black Prince) in 1361.

Queen Victoria was to take no part in the ceremony. Dressed in black she would walk alone to the closet of Catherine of Aragon, set high above the choir of the chapel, from where she could privately view the proceedings below. Members of the royal family were informed that mourning restrictions were not lifted and lilac and white, or white and grey dresses would be required. However, matters were relaxed with regard to the bride and she donned a fashionable court dress described as a 'petticoat of white satin trimmed with chatelaines of orange blossom, myrtle and bouffantes of tulle, Honiton lace, and bouquets of orange blossom and myrtle'.

The bride's outfit provided the royal family with a welcome opportunity to boost native manufacturers, once again. Princess Alexandra, who had been given a beautiful dress of Brussels lace by King Leopold of the Belgians as a wedding present, found it was considered quite inappropriate for use as a wedding dress. Instead a dress of English silk was made by Mrs James, a favoured dressmaker in London. It was lavishly trimmed with Honiton lace, made with a design of

Above:
Wedding favours celebrating the marriage of the Prince and Princess of Wales.

Left:
Albert Edward, Prince of Wales, and Alexandra, Princess of Wales on their wedding day, 10 March 1863.

Right:
Princess Alexandra's wedding dress, 1863.

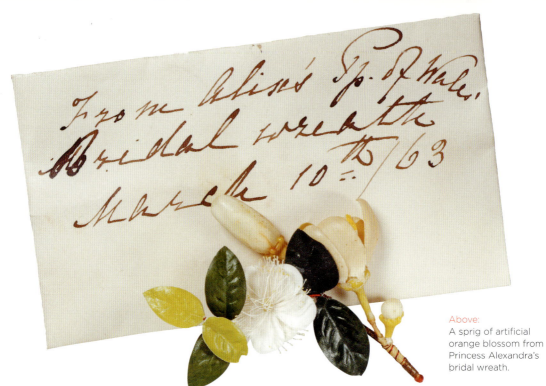

From aliss's Pss of Wales Bridal wreath March 10 th/63

Above:
A sprig of artificial orange blossom from Princess Alexandra's bridal wreath.

Below:
The Prince and Princess of Wales's wedding cake.

cornucopias, from which tumbled roses, shamrock and thistles. A veil was made to match.

The dress was very promptly remodelled after the wedding, perhaps in an attempt to boost the small trousseau of the Princess. The skirt of the dress, as it survives today, has been made out of the court train of silver moire that once completed the wedding ensemble. Happily, the garlands of wax orange blossom and the spectacular lace flounces and veil have been carefully preserved.

The Princess was allowed eight bridesmaids, matching the number that had attended the Princess Royal earlier. They were all the eldest daughters of peers. Another link to the earlier wedding was the inclusion in the wedding bouquet of a small sprig of myrtle taken from a bush grown from a sprig carried by the Princess Royal. This was a German custom. This myrtle bush and its successors have supplied royal brides until the present

day. On beholding his bride, in all her finery, the Prince of Wales likened her to a 'Rustic Goddess', but his own attire was similarly splendid. Like many royal bridegrooms he favoured military uniform and wore that of an army general. Over this were placed the traditional flowing dark blue robes of the Order of the Garter.

The event was judged by all observers to be most magnificent – as were some of the guests. It was reported that the Duchess of Westminster wore over half a million pounds worth of jewels, almost matching the splendid attire of the Maharaja Dhuleep Singh and his wife. Lady Spence caused a considerable stir when she arrived in a dress reputed to have belonged to Queen Marie Antoinette.

Below:
William Powell Frith, *The Marriage of the Prince of Wales, 10 March 1863*. Queen Victoria can be seen watching the ceremony from a closet above the congregation.

Above:
From left to right: Princess Helena, Princess Beatrice and Princess Louise wearing mourning dress at the wedding of the Prince and Princess of Wales in 1863.

Queen Mary

(1867-1953)

The engagement of Princess Mary to Prince George (later King George V) gave 'the greatest satisfaction' to his grandmother Queen Victoria and much pleasure to the nation when the couple married in 1893.

Queen Victoria had 40 grandchildren, who would marry into almost every royal family in Europe. The Queen took an immense interest in these alliances, but perhaps her greatest concern was to ensure that there would be good and happy matches for the children of the Prince and Princess of Wales, through whom the succession to the throne of Great Britain would be secured.

Their eldest son was Prince Albert Victor who, after a series of unsatisfactory attachments, became engaged to Princess Victoria Mary (known affectionately as Princess May), daughter of the Duke and Duchess of Teck. Their wedding was set for 27 February 1892, but on 14 January the Prince died of influenza.

Prince George, second son of the Prince and Princess of Wales, suddenly found himself heir to both his father and the throne of Great Britain and his matrimonial plans assumed a national importance. His name was soon coupled with that of Princess Mary and in May 1893 Prince George, recently created Duke of York, proposed. Queen Victoria recorded in her journal, 'I have so much wished for this engagement that it gives me the greatest satisfaction'.

Just a few days later, Prince George met his grandmother to discuss plans for the wedding. It was decided that the date should be 6 July 1893 and that the bridesmaids should be the sisters of the groom: princesses Victoria and Maud of Wales, and eight little nieces. In view of the fact that the recent funeral of Prince Albert Victor had been held in St George's Chapel, Windsor, the Chapel Royal at St James's Palace was chosen as the venue, despite the misgivings of the Queen, who considered it 'small and very ugly'.

Following the lead of Queen Victoria and the Princess of Wales, Princess Mary was to ensure that materials employed within her wedding ensemble were of English manufacture. Having selected a fabric design – consisting of silver bunches of flowers 'typical of Britain and Ireland', tied together with a true lovers' knot, on a white ground – she took a keen interest in the manufacturing details as it was woven up in Spitalfields. The dress was made by

Linton and Curtis of 16 Albermarle Street, and took the form of a court dress, as had become conventional. *The Lady* describes it as being of:

'a very rich white satin...brocaded with silver...the long, plain train looked as if it were perfectly capable of standing alone, and just the front of the skirt was of white satin. It was edged with three tiny satin flounces trimmed with silver, and above these were three flounces of the beautiful Honiton point-lace...a trail of orange blossom on each side separated this satin front with its lace...The bodice was of silver brocade with the floral design so placed as to form its sole ornament, with the exception of the Honiton point round the neck and the wreath of orange blossoms over it, with small bouquets on the breast and shoulders.'

Above:
Prince Albert Victor and Princess Mary of Teck, 1891. The couple were planning their wedding when the Prince died suddenly in 1892.

Far left:
The Duke and Duchess of York on their wedding day, 6 July 1893.

Left:
Princess Mary's wedding dress, 1893.

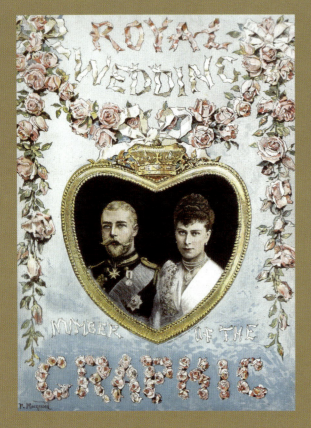

Above:
The front cover of *The Graphic*, celebrating the marriage of Prince George and Princess Mary.

Below:
These diamond brooches were wedding gifts to the bride from the Inhabitants of Kensington and the County of Dorset.

Treasured sets of royal wedding lace were often lent to the brides of a later generation as tokens of affection and in celebration of the continuity of the royal line. Princess Mary wore, arranged over her petticoat, the lace flounces, with their distinctive pattern of flower-filled cornucopias, which had been worn by her mother Princess Mary Adelaide for her wedding in 1866. These were the flounces originally made for the Princess of Wales in 1863. Her wedding veil, claimed the Press, was also worn attached to a small wreath of orange blossom.

The Lady described the dresses worn by the 'little maids' as 'short white satin frocks with chiffon flounces headed by silver lace, and the tops of the bodices were prettily puffed with chiffon under which the silver lace was laid'. The dresses of the older bridesmaids were made of the same materials but the bodices, trimmed with a larger-scale silver lace, had pointed basques and long sleeves. They were made up by Linton and Curtis, the makers of the bride's wedding dress. The silk satin came from Spitalfields at Princess Mary's express request.

Princess Mary carefully monitored the assembly of her trousseau to ensure that goods were obtained from a broad range of manufacturers. She claimed, 'we get trousseau things sent to us on approval from all parts of England, Scotland and Ireland so that we are nearly driven mad and have not a moment's peace'.

Since the death of Prince Albert Victor there had been much popular sympathy for Princess Mary, which was transformed to delight as plans for her marriage to Prince George were announced. She received many spectacular and valuable presents including a diamond tiara from the County of Surrey and a ruby and diamond bracelet from the County of Cornwall. Perhaps the most unusual was the presentation by Mr Searcy of a magnificent wedding cake and, as Tsarevich Nicholas of Russia reported to his mother, 'Somebody even managed to present them with a cow'!

The crowds turned out in their thousands to witness the wedding processions, as they made their way under the triumphal arches, garlands and banners, which marked the route between Buckingham Palace and St James's Palace on 6 July. 'The loyalty and enthusiasm was immense', reported Queen Victoria. At half past eleven, the procession of the bridegroom set out. Prince George was observed to be wearing naval uniform, over which hung the Collar of the Order of the Garter. He was supported by his father and his uncle, Prince Alfred, Duke of Edinburgh. The procession of Queen Victoria followed, the Queen wearing 'in honour of occasion my wedding lace over a light black stuff, and my wedding veil surmounted by a small coronet'. The greatest attraction, however, proved to be the procession of the bride.

Above:
Princess Mary choosing her wedding trousseau by Arthur Hopkins, 1893.

Right:
This ruby and diamond bracelet was presented to Princess Mary by the County of Cornwall.

Below:
Wedding favours made to celebrate the marriage of the Duke and Duchess of York, 1893.

On the occasion of the wedding procession of the Duke & Duchess of York. July. 6. 1893. The Baroness Burdett Coutts accommodated at her house in Stratton Street, which overlooked the route, as many children as she could. These favors were distributed. — All Mr. Kendal's children received them

The ceremony was witnessed by a huge number of guests crowded into the Chapel Royal; the gentlemen were dressed in 'uniform or full dress with trousers', and the ladies in 'full dress without trains or plumes'. The chapel had been made to look very splendid. Decked with red and white flowers gathered from the gardens of the royal residences of Osborne and Frogmore, the chapel was hung with tapestries taken from Kensington Palace.

After the ceremony the company retired to Buckingham Palace where a wedding breakfast was served for 400 guests. 'It had all been very prettily arranged', concluded Queen Victoria as she toasted the bride and bridegroom. Prince George and his new bride were crowned King George V and Queen Mary on 22 June 1911.

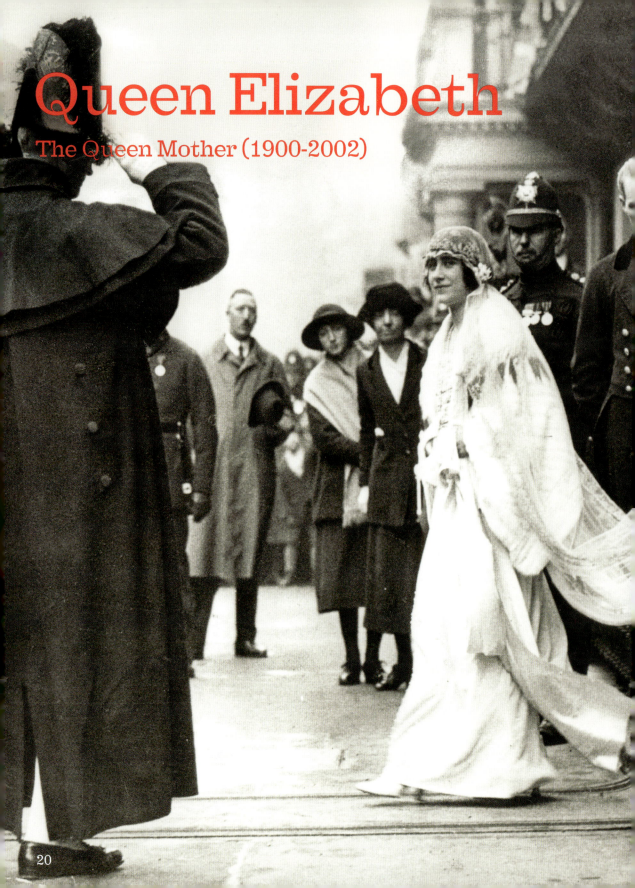

Queen Elizabeth

The Queen Mother (1900-2002)

The Duke of York and Lady Elizabeth Bowes-Lyon were married in Westminster Abbey on a wet April morning in 1923. The Duke later recorded in his diary 'the sun actually came out as Elizabeth entered the Abbey'.

With the outbreak of the First World War in 1914, came many changes in society. In 1918, when the country emerged from the war, many European royal dynasties had been swept away, and for the five surviving children of King George V and Queen Mary finding a suitable spouse proved an anxious task. Princess Mary was the first to marry in 1922. Her choice was Henry, Viscount Lascelles, a suitably well-connected English aristocrat. Amongst her bridesmaids was the pretty, vivacious Lady Elizabeth Bowes-Lyon, daughter of the Earl of Strathmore. She caught the eye of the King's second son, Prince Albert, Duke of York. After some deliberation she agreed to marry him. The date for the wedding was set for 26 April 1923.

With memories of the war still very vivid, the Duke of York had chosen to wear on his wedding day, the uniform of the Royal Air Force, with whom he had trained at Cranwell. Other royal principals wore the full dress of various services. The King was in his uniform as Admiral of the Fleet, the Prince of Wales wore the full dress uniform of the Grenadier Guards, while Prince Henry of Gloucester chose naval uniform and Prince George of Kent wore naval cadet's dress. Uniforms were also worn by many of the guests.

Above:
Detail of the bead embroidery on the wedding dress worn by Queen Elizabeth The Queen Mother.

Left:
The wedding dress of Queen Elizabeth The Queen Mother, 1923.

Far left:
Lady Elizabeth Bowes-Lyon leaving her London home for her wedding to the Duke of York, 26 April 1923.

Right:
This miniature of Lady Elizabeth Bowes-Lyon by Mabel Hankey was a wedding gift to the Duke of York from the bride's mother.

Below:
A group of rain-soaked spectators waiting to see the bride and groom.

The bride's dress was described by *The Times* as, 'the simplest ever made for a royal wedding'. It was of chiffon moire, which had been specially dyed to match the colour of the *point de Flanders* lace veil, lent by Queen Mary. The dress had a deep, square neckline with a narrow piped edge. The bodice was cut straight to the waist, with no darts, and the back extended to a separate train. At the front, the skirt was gently pleated into the waist seam. Down the front of the dress was an appliquéd bar of silver lamé with horizontal bars arranged over the bodice to form the appearance of a stomacher; each bar was decorated and edged with gold embroidery and pearl and paste beads. Integral to the dress was a train that extended 10 inches beyond the hem and spread 80 inches wide, over which was a train of tulle edged with lace lent by Queen Mary.

The veil was secured by a simple wreath of myrtle leaves, with knots of white roses – the emblem of the County of York – and white heather.

Lady Elizabeth's bouquet included roses and lilies-of-the-valley, with a white rose at either side. Her shoes were of ivory silk moire and embroidered with silver roses. There were eight bridesmaids, all wearing simple dresses: underdresses of *crêpe de chine* with bands of Nottingham lace, covered with white chiffon.

Lady Elizabeth made her way with her attendants to Westminster Abbey, pausing to lay her bouquet on the Tomb of the Unknown Warrior in honour of the war dead. Echoing this gesture, at the conclusion of her funeral in 2002, the Queen's wreath was taken from the top of her coffin

and laid on the tomb as her final acknowledgement of the sacrifice. If this gesture in 1923 looked back to the war, in the technology that reported the event there were glimmers of the shape of things to come. In addition to the coverage in newspapers and magazines, for the first time cinema films were made of the ceremony and were available for viewing on the very evening of the wedding day.

Following the abdication in 1936 of Edward VIII, Prince Albert's elder brother, the couple were proclaimed King and Queen and Prince Albert took the name George VI. George VI and Queen Elizabeth had two children, Princess Elizabeth and Princess Margaret, born in 1926 and 1930.

Above:
The wedding ceremony of Lady Elizabeth Bowes-Lyon and the Duke of York in Westminster Abbey.

Below:
The Duke and Duchess of York with their bridesmaids on the day of their wedding.

Queen Elizabeth II

(1926-)

'It is with great pleasure that the King and Queen announce the betrothal of their dearly beloved daughter The Princess Elizabeth to Lieutenant Philip Mountbatten RN.'

On 9 July 1947, the *Court Circular* published the above announcement, which put post-war Britain into a flurry of excitement. The country was impoverished after a second world war; society had changed. The wedding of the King's eldest daughter was to provide a herald of better times to come.

The wedding ceremony was to take place in Westminster Abbey on 20 November and preparations continued throughout the summer and into the autumn. The bridesmaids and the pages were all to be relatives, with the exception of Lady Elizabeth Lambert, whose family had particularly close connections with the court. The others were Princess Margaret, Princess Alexandra, Lady Caroline Montagu-Douglas-Scott, Lady Mary Cambridge, the Honourable Pamela Mountbatten, Miss Diana Bowes-Lyon and the Honourable Margaret Elphinstone. The two pages were princes Michael of Kent and William of Gloucester, both aged 5.

Presents from parts of the Empire represented their home products: a beaver coat from Canada, silver dishes from Australia and lace from Malta. The presents were both useful as well as beautiful: the people of Leamington Spa sent an electric washing machine, the Women's Voluntary Service, a refrigerator and, concerned by what she had heard about food rationing in England, an American child had a live turkey delivered to Buckingham Palace. After the wedding, many of these gifts were put on public display at St James's Palace.

All of the plans came to fruition on 20 November. At 11.16am, Princess Elizabeth left Buckingham Palace with the King and drove to Westminster Abbey in the Irish State Coach. The procession drove down The Mall, through Admiralty Arch and along Whitehall. Although post-war austerity had limited the decorations, the number of spectators who filled the streets along the route was greater than ever before.

Above:
The official engagement photograph of Princess Elizabeth and Prince Philip by Dorothy Wilding, July 1947.

Below:
Princess Elizabeth's wedding dress, 1947.

Princess Elizabeth photographed by Baron on her wedding day, 20 November 1947.

Princess Elizabeth and the Duke of Edinburgh with their attendants and family, photographed in the Throne Room at Buckingham Palace on their wedding day.

Inside the Abbey, along with rows of distinguished guests, waited the Duke of Edinburgh, his naval uniform decorated with medal ribbons, the Star of the Order of the Garter, to which he had been appointed the previous day, and the Greek Order of the Redeemer.

Princess Elizabeth's dress had been made by Norman Hartnell, a young talented couturier who had been introduced to Queen Elizabeth and her daughters in 1935. He had designed the wedding dress worn by Princess Alice at her marriage to Prince Henry, Duke of Gloucester, the King's brother. The commission included bridesmaids dresses trimmed with pink tulle for princesses Elizabeth and Margaret. The success of this project led to many later royal commissions.

Hartnell had been asked to submit designs for Princess Elizabeth's wedding dress soon after the engagement was announced and by the middle of August learnt he had been given the prestigious commission, with less than three months to make the dress and train.

In his anxious search for inspiration for the dress of a future queen, Hartnell came across an image of Primavera by Botticelli in a London art gallery. This figure – with its trailing garlands of jasmine, smilax, syringa and rose-like blossoms – was derived from the classical goddess of flowers, Flora, and its floral attributes suggested to him the promise of growth and new beginnings after the drabness of the war and post-war era. The royal commission, however, prevented him from undertaking a scheduled visit to the United States where he knew he could obtain the supplies he needed. He sent instead his manager, Captain Mitchison. When asked if he had anything to declare on his return, Captain Mitchison replied that he had indeed – 10,000 pearls for Princess Elizabeth's wedding dress.

The dress – in its 4-foot-long box – was eventually delivered to Buckingham Palace on the eve of the wedding,

already the subject of intense speculation. Although Hartnell whitewashed the windows of his workroom, some aspects of the design were inevitably leaked out. The dress was still, however, a triumph. Made of satin, it was a one-piece princess style with a fitted bodice, the neckline having a deep-scalloped edge. The front bodice was cut in three panels and the back was cut in four, fastening down the centre back with buttons and loops. The wrist-length, tight-fitting sleeves ended in embroidered cuffs. From the low-pointed waist, the skirt, cut on the cross, extended to a deep circular train.

At the shoulder there were three covered loops to attach the train. Even after the war Hartnell was clearly still working on tradition, established years before, of royal wedding dresses that demanded a court train. Princess Elizabeth's was to be 15-feet long. The train was decorated with white roses in padded satin and corn in diamanté and pearl embroidery. Additional flower

Above:
A special royal wedding edition of *Picture Post* magazine, showing Princess Elizabeth arriving at Westminster Abbey in the Irish State Coach.

Right:
Princess Elizabeth and the Duke of Edinburgh had 12 official wedding cakes. As food rationing was still in force, they were made from ingredients sent to the Princess from overseas.

Below:
A silver-painted decoration from one of the wedding cakes.

motifs were included and Hartnell's vision of Primavera was built up with orange blossom, syringa and jasmine. His predilection for tulle over lace was expressed in the long veil, which was held in place by a diamond tiara. Princess Elizabeth's bouquet, which was briefly misplaced at the palace on the morning of the wedding, was supplied by the Worshipful Company of Gardeners. It was composed of white orchids, with a sprig of myrtle taken, as was traditional, from the bush grown from Princess Victoria's bouquet.

With the delivery of the dress to the palace, Hartnell's work for the wedding was by no means over. He had been commissioned to design and make the dresses for the bridesmaids as well. Instead of Botticelli, he looked to the royal collection of Victorian pictures by Winterhalter, Tuxen and Hayter, for inspiration. The dresses he designed were of ivory silk tulle with a tightly-fitted bodice, the shoulders swathed with a deep *fichu* of pearl-spotted tulle which, in a reference to the bride's dress, was decorated with a trail of appliqué white-satin syringa. The skirt was embroidered with clusters of this flower. The bridesmaids wore wreaths of miniature wheatsheaves, lilies-of-the-valley and London Pride – made of white satin and silver lamé – and carried bouquets of white orchids, lilies-of-the-valley, gardenias, white bouvardia, white roses and nerine. The two pages wore Royal Stuart tartan kilts with frilled white shirts and lace jabots.

Above:
Princess Elizabeth and the Duke of Edinburgh leaving Westminster Abbey after their wedding ceremony.

Below:
A vast crowd gathered to catch a glimpse of the newly-weds.

Princess Margaret

(1930-2002)

Princess Margaret, an acclaimed beauty and one of the most fashionable women in London, did not disappoint on her wedding day in May 1960. 'It seems as if she moved in a soft white cloud', gushed *The Times*, describing her Norman Hartnell gown.

Norman Hartnell was asked to undertake the commission for the wedding of Princess Margaret and Antony Armstrong-Jones, a successful photographer, which took place at Westminster Abbey on 6 May 1960. His designs were much admired by the Princess who explained: he was 'always so good at getting the balance right'.

Simplicity was the keynote of Hartnell's design for the bride's dress, which suited the Princess's taste and was stunningly effective. As *The Times* remarked, 'It seems as if she moved in a soft white cloud'. This effect was due in part to the 30 yards of fine diaphanous silk that comprised the upper layer of the dress alone. The fitted bodice had a V-neck and the skirt flared out in 12 panels. A deep inverted pleat let into the waist at the centre back allowed the dress to be folded out when the bride sat down and then fall back into place so that no unsightly creases would show.

The shape of the skirt was produced by the petticoat, constructed from eight layers of silk net. Additional flounces of stiff net ensured that it stood out each side in the form of a *robe de style*. There was no separate court train, although the dress itself was trained. The veil was made by St Cyr of Paris and the flowers included the traditional myrtle. The Princess's shoes were made by Edward Rayne in a court style, of white crepe faced with satin and with slender 2 ½ inch heels.

Princess Diana

(1961-97)

On 2 July 1981 the *Daily Express* reported that the 'whole world stopped for the wedding' of the Prince of Wales and Lady Diana Spencer.

The wedding of the heir to the throne was an extraordinary media event with over 80 broadcasting organisations from 50 countries taking live pictures from the BBC. It was the first time a Prince of Wales had married for over 100 years but that does not really explain why millions of people across the globe were glued to their televisions: it was more to do with wanting to be part of the romance of the occasion; the climax of the fairy-tale.

It was the genius of David and Elizabeth Emmanuel, who were chosen to design the bride's dress, to reflect the fairy-tale. Lady Diana's choice of this young couple was a break with tradition although she had worn some of their designs before – notably a black strapless evening gown in which she appeared for her first official engagement following the announcement of the forthcoming marriage. It was considered by some to be too revealing and did not reappear.

Above:
A set of stamps was issued to commemorate the royal wedding.

Right:
Diana, Princess of Wales photographed by Lord Lichfield at Buckingham Palace after her wedding.

Below:
Lady Diana arrives at St Paul's Cathedral, the train of her dress streaming behind her.

Above:
Charles and Diana's wedding inspired hundreds of commemorative gifts from T-shirts and tea towels to mugs and biscuit tins.

Right:
The Prince and Princess of Wales leaving St Paul's Cathedral following their wedding ceremony. Diana's bouquet was later laid on the Tomb of the Unknown Soldier in Westminster Abbey – a tradition begun by Queen Elizabeth The Queen Mother in 1923.

Naturally, intense speculation surrounded the design of the wedding dress – one MP hoped that the couple would be married wearing blue jeans giving a boost to the manufacture of British denim. The Emmanuels felt besieged in their studio, where the window blinds were drawn and no sketches were made. They wanted to transform the shy young girl into a fairy-tale princess and in this they triumphed. When Lady Diana emerged from her carriage at the foot of the steps of St Paul's Cathedral, Jean Rook, writing in the *Daily Express* described the bride as 'one great creamery ivory thrill', although other commentators remarked unkindly on the tendency of the material to crease.

The dress had a fitted bodice with a deep flounce around the neckline and Carrickmacross lace panels at the front and back decorated with mother-of-pearl sequins. A lace flounce gathered the full sleeves and from the waist flowed a train nearly 25 feet long. The skirt billowed out, supported by a crinoline petticoat made up of layers of ivory tulle and nylon net. Because a bride should always wear something blue to bring her good fortune a small blue bow was sewn into the waistband.

As she walked up the aisle Lady Diana had her face veiled in ivory silk tulle, glinting with hand-embroidered mother-of-pearl sequins, the veil

secured by the Spencer diamond tiara. She left the cathedral a royal princess, her veil drawn back, carrying a bouquet of flowers given by the Worshipful Company of Gardeners, which included, by tradition, a sprig of myrtle. Now she was supported on the arm of her husband. He wore the full dress uniform of a commander in the Royal Navy, the coat of blue Venetian cloth with two rows of six buttons down the front. On his chest were pinned the stars of the orders of the Garter, Thistle and Bath: fairy-tale dress and tradition reassuringly linked together.

Behind the bride were five bridesmaids, all wearing dresses that reflected the design of the bride's but in a lighter weight silk, and two pages wearing miniature full dress naval uniforms from the mid-19th century – again fairy-tale and tradition linked together.

Memories of that July day in 1981 have been kept fresh in the minds of millions, not least through the commemorative souvenirs that were manufactured in huge quantities and the videos that were, for the first time, available.

But the most persistent memory for many must still be that dress, emerging in its ivory glory from the carriage at St Paul's. It was once more, the dress that made the day. And it was, after all, as the *Evening Standard* reported 'the wedding of the century'.

Camilla, Duchess of Cornwall

(1947-)

For her marriage to the Prince of Wales, Camilla Parker-Bowles had the difficult task of selecting not one but two bridal outfits: one for the ceremony itself and one for the blessing. The elegant dresses and dramatic headdresses that she chose were acclaimed as 'faultless, perfect and right'.

On 9 April 2005, following his divorce from Princess Diana in 1996 and her tragic death in 1997, Prince Charles married Camilla Parker-Bowles. Second marriages are by no means unusual in society as a whole, but they present the bride with a different set of options when it comes to choosing her wedding dress.

Above:
The Prince of Wales and the Duchess of Cornwall following their marriage ceremony at Windsor Guildhall.

Below:
The Prince of Wales and the Duchess of Cornwall on their wedding day, photographed with their parents and children.

The wedding itself took place in Windsor Guildhall, and was a civil occasion as Camilla was divorced. The bride wore an afternoon dress and coat made by the design duo Robinson Valentine. The coat of oyster-coloured silk, woven with a basket-work pattern, perfectly complemented the cream chiffon dress worn beneath, which was decorated round the hem with a fringe of large cream sequins. The outfit was completed with a dramatic hat trimmed with lace and feathers made by the Irish milliner, Philip Treacy. Rather than wearing military uniform, Prince Charles chose elegant morning dress, in keeping with the nature of the occasion.

The Prince wore the same morning dress at the blessing of the marriage which followed at St George's Chapel, Windsor Castle. As a gentle gesture he changed the colour of the flower in his buttonhole so that it would complement his bride's dress. Camilla's outfit for the blessing was also by Robinson Valentine. It comprised a full-length dress of pale blue chiffon embroidered with gold, in a design taken from a piece of jewellery that had been in the collection of Camilla's mother. Over the dress she wore a coat of blue and gold damask. Philip Treacy made her a magnificent headdress – a halo of golden feathers.

The fashion designer Jasper Conran commented: 'The clothes were faultless, perfect and right'. Hamish Bowles, European Editor at Large for *Vogue* added: 'It is quite clear she is not going to be restricted to the timid gesture and is prepared to make a glamorous, flamboyantly faultless statement, when the occasion demands'.

Left:
The Duchess of Cornwall carried a small posy of lilies-of-the-valley mixed with primroses and myrtle, designed by Shane Connolly.

Catherine, Duchess of Cambridge
(1982-)

Despite intense speculation, Catherine Middleton and her designer managed to keep this remarkable dress a secret until the wedding day.

'It's a fashion moment!' exclaimed the BBC commentator on Friday 29 April 2011. Miss Catherine Middleton, shortly to become HRH The Duchess of Cambridge, stepped from the Rolls Royce that had driven her and her father from the

Right:
Catherine Middleton arrives at the Abbey looking radiant in her Alexander McQueen gown.

Below:
The Duke and Duchess of Cambridge pose in the Throne Room at Buckingham Palace with their bridesmaids and page boys for the official wedding photographs by Hugo Burnand.

Goring Hotel to Westminster Abbey, where Prince William of Wales was waiting for her. At last everyone had the answer to that question – what would her wedding dress look like?

The dress had to fulfil the expectations of millions of people and also echo the conventions long established for royal wedding dresses, including the use of British materials and skills. It succeeded brilliantly. Designed by Sarah Burton at Alexander McQueen the dress was of ivory satin, the bodice boned and the hips padded, with a full skirt and a modest train of just under 9 foot. The lace, made by the Royal School of Needlework, at Hampton Court Palace, was handworked using the Carrickmacross lace-making technique, which originated in Ireland in the 1820s. It included roses, thistles and shamrock in its design. With the dress Miss Middleton wore a Cartier halo diamond tiara, lent by The Queen,

which had been given to the then Princess Elizabeth by her mother on the occasion of her 18th birthday. Miss Middleton's diamond earrings were a present from her parents and featured a design of oak leaves and acorns, which are also part of the new Middleton coat of arms. Her bouquet, which included Sweet William and the traditional myrtle, would later be placed on the Tomb of the Unknown Warrior, itself a tradition of royal weddings dating back to the marriage of the Duke of York and Lady Elizabeth Bowes-Lyon in 1923.

The sense of duty that this last gesture implied was also evident in the military and naval uniforms worn by many of the male members of both the British and European royal families present. Prince William wore the ceremonial uniform of the Irish Guards, the regiment of which The Queen appointed him Colonel in February 2011. The regiment was formed in 1900 and is distinguished by the shamrock on the collar and the fact that the buttons are arranged in fours, to denote it is the fourth Foot Guards regiment; it was not possible to see this distinction as Prince William also wore the sash of the Order of the Garter, mounted with the Wings of the Royal Air Force. His best man, Prince Harry, was in the uniform of a Captain of the Blues and Royals, part of the Household Cavalry. The bride's attendants echoed the desire to promote British design and the country's military heritage. The bridesmaids were in dresses by Nicki Macfarlane and her daughter Charlotte, while the page boys wore a re-creation of Foot Guards officers' uniforms of the early 19th century, made by Kashket and partners. Miss Middleton's sister, Philippa, chose a full-length, figure-hugging dress by Sarah Burton in ivory satin crepe for her role as maid of honour. It was embellished with the same button detail and lace trims as the bride's dress.

Left:
The Duke and Duchess of Cambridge emerge from Westminster Abbey as husband and wife.

There were few surprises in the dress worn by male guests. In spite of early rumours to the contrary the Prime Minister, David Cameron, did wear morning dress. His wife, Samantha, on the other hand, occasioned comment because she did not appear wearing a hat, unlike the other female guests. There were some interesting styles in headdress and particular comment afterwards centred on the Philip Treacy hats worn by princesses Beatrice and Eugenie.

After the ceremony, the new Duchess of Cambridge walked back down the aisle with her husband, performing a perfect curtsey to The Queen and emerging from the Abbey as the perfect consort to the second in line to the throne.

The use of the 1902 State Landau for the journey to Buckingham Palace emphasised what are perhaps the greatest assets of the British monarchy – its openness and accessibility combined with its strong sense of tradition and heritage. One voice from the crowd, overheard on the television coverage, summed up the feeling that the Royal Family belong to the nation and vice versa: 'Kate's a treasure for the country now'.

Above:
In addition to the Cartier halo tiara, lent by The Queen, the Duchess of Cambridge wore diamond oak leaf and acorn earrings, a gift from her parents on her wedding day.

Family tree

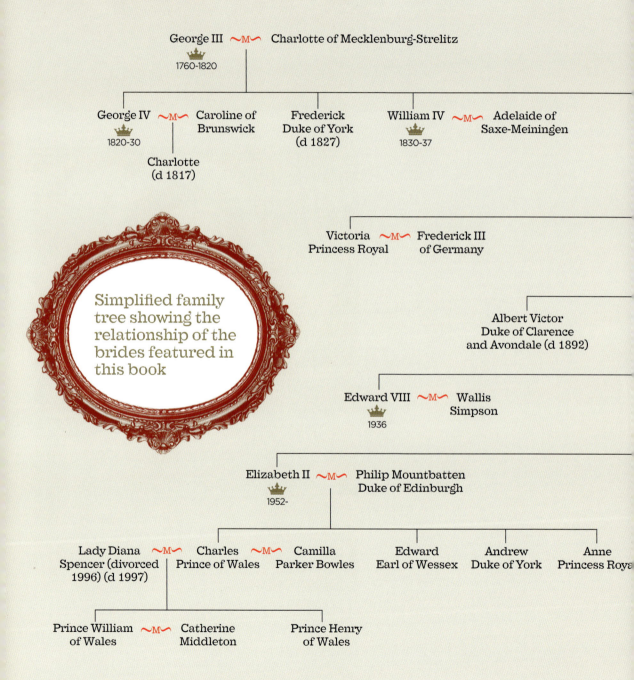

George III ~M~ Charlotte of Mecklenburg-Strelitz
1760-1820

George IV ~M~ Caroline of Brunswick
1820-30

Charlotte (d 1817)

Frederick Duke of York (d 1827)

William IV ~M~ Adelaide of Saxe-Meiningen
1830-37

Victoria Princess Royal ~M~ Frederick III of Germany

Simplified family tree showing the relationship of the brides featured in this book

Albert Victor Duke of Clarence and Avondale (d 1892)

Edward VIII ~M~ Wallis Simpson
1936

Elizabeth II ~M~ Philip Mountbatten Duke of Edinburgh
1952-

Lady Diana Spencer (divorced 1996) (d 1997) ~M~ Charles Prince of Wales ~M~ Camilla Parker Bowles

Edward Earl of Wessex

Andrew Duke of York

Anne Princess Roya

Prince William of Wales ~M~ Catherine Middleton

Prince Henry of Wales

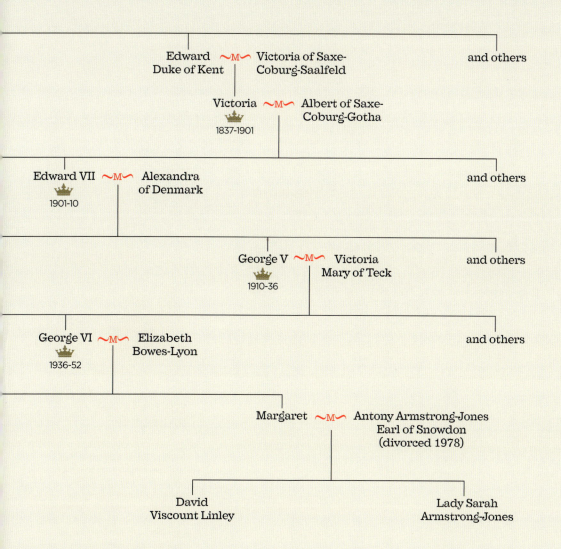

Edward
Duke of Kent
~M~ Victoria of Saxe-
Coburg-Saalfeld
and others

Victoria ~M~ Albert of Saxe-
Coburg-Gotha
1837-1901

Edward VII ~M~ Alexandra
of Denmark
1901-10
and others

George V ~M~ Victoria
Mary of Teck
1910-36
and others

George VI ~M~ Elizabeth
Bowes-Lyon
1936-52
and others

Margaret ~M~ Antony Armstrong-Jones
Earl of Snowdon
(divorced 1978)

David
Viscount Linley

Lady Sarah
Armstrong-Jones

Acknowledgements

Published by Historic Royal Palaces,
Hampton Court Palace, Surrey, KT8 9AU

© Historic Royal Palaces, 2011

ISBN 978-1-873993-23-1

Written by Nigel Arch and Joanna Marschner
Edited by Clare Murphy
Picture research by Annie Heron and Louise Nash
Designed by www.brandremedy.com
Printed by BKT

Illustrations

Abbreviations: b = bottom, c = centre, l = left, r = right, t = top

AFP/Getty Images: page 41t; Hugo Burnand/Clarence
House: page 38; Camera Press, London: pages 25, 26-7
(Bassano), 29t, 30 (Cecil Beaton), 31; © City of London: page
10tl; Getty Images: pages 3, 7t, 22b, 28t, 29b, 36t; Vivian
Hutcheson: page 35t; Illustrated London News Ltd/
Mary Evans: page 18t; Susan Jenkins: page 34l; Keystone
Archives/Heritage Images: page 34r; Lichfield/Getty Images:
pages 33, 35b; Museum of London: page 7b; National
Portrait Gallery, London: pages 6, 17t, 23b; Christopher
Pledger/*The Daily Telegraph*: front cover, page 39;
Popperfoto/Getty Images: pages 20-21; Press Association:
pages 36b, 37, 40, 41b, back cover; Rex Features: pages 4-5;
The Royal Collection © 2011, Her Majesty Queen Elizabeth II:
pages 1, 2, 8l, 8b, 9, 10tr, 10cl, 10b, 11, 12, 13t, 13b, 14t, 14b, 15t,
15b, 17b, 18b, 19t, 19c, 19b, 21bl, 21br, 22t, 23t, 24t, 24b, 28bl,
28br; Leonard de Selva/CORBIS: page 32t; Topfoto: page 16;
Topfoto/Woodmansterne: page 32b.

FRONT COVER: Catherine Middleton arrives at Westminster
Abbey, 29 April 2011.
PAGE 1: A silver-painted decoration from one of Princess
Elizabeth's wedding cakes, 1947.
BACK COVER: The Duke and Duchess of Cambridge
surprised the crowds on their wedding day in April 2011
by making an appearance in a convertible Aston Martin.

www.hrp.org.uk

Glossary

Appliqué: a style of embroidery used on fabric, lace, leather,
etc in which cutout motifs are applied to another surface.

Basque: the continuation of an upper garment below the
waist, creating a type of short skirt.

Chatelaine: an ornamental chain worn by women at the waist.

Diaphanous: perfectly transparent.

Fichu: a triangular scarf of light textile worn by women as
a covering for the neck and shoulders.

Jabot: a frill worn generally by men to conceal the front
fastening of a shirt.

Lamé: a textile woven with a weft of metallic thread.

Moire: a silk or synthetic silk impressed with a wavy or
watered pattern, created by passing the textile between
rollers engraved with the design.

Robe de style: a type of dress popular in the 1920s and
1930s having a tight bodice and bouffant skirt supported
with stiffened petticoats over the hips.

Stomacher: a separate decorative triangular panel forming
the front of a woman's low-necked bodice.

Tulle: fine net or gauze made of silk or cotton.

Measurements
Yards, feet and inches are used in the text as most of
the dresses were made using the imperial system of
measurement. For the purposes of conversion:

1 yard = 0.9144 metre, 1 foot = 0.3048 metre,
1 inch = 0.0254 metre

Historic Royal PALACES

Historic Royal Palaces is the
independent charity that looks
after the Tower of London,
Hampton Court Palace, the
Banqueting House, Kensington
Palace and Kew Palace. We help
everyone explore the story of
how monarchs and people have
shaped society, in some of the
greatest palaces ever built.

We receive no funding from the
Government or the Crown, so
we depend on the support of
our visitors, members, donors,
volunteers and sponsors.